UNIVERSITY OF MINNESOTA

Frank Norris

BY W. M. FROHOCK

UNIVERSITY OF MINNESOTA PRESS · MINNEAPOLIS

Printed in the United States of America at
the North Central Publishing Company, St. Paul

Library of Congress Catalog Card Number: 68-64751

PUBLISHED IN GREAT BRITAIN, INDIA, AND PAKISTAN BY THE OXFORD
UNIVERSITY PRESS, LONDON, BOMBAY, AND KARACHI, AND IN CANADA
BY THE COPP CLARK PUBLISHING CO. LIMITED, TORONTO

FRANK NORRIS

W. M. FROHOCK teaches French and comparative literature at Harvard. His books include *The Novel of Violence in America* and *Style and Temper: Studies in French Fiction.*

⌁ *Frank Norris*

FRANK NORRIS' name is much better known today than anything he ever wrote. The manuals of American literature bestow measured praise on *McTeague* (1899) and *The Octopus* (1901), note that *The Pit* (1903) was a relative failure, and mention the posthumous *Vandover and the Brute* (1914). They go on to report that Norris introduced French naturalism into American fiction, discovered the talent of Theodore Dreiser, and influenced legislation designed to curb the railroad monopolies.

A more complete account would have to include a long, pseudo-romantic narrative in verse called *Yvernelle: A Legend of Feudal France* (published in 1892 while Norris was an undergraduate), a sheaf of short stories, enough literary criticism to fill a volume, and three more novels: *Moran of the Lady Letty* (1898), *A Man's Woman* (1899), and *Blix* (1899). No more can be said for *Moran* than that it is as entertaining as many of Jack London's stories, and no more implausible; even less can be said for *A Man's Woman*; but the total achievement is considerable for a writer who died at thirty-two. He did not exert the general influence on American letters of a Howells, and his work has attracted no circle of admirers like Stephen Crane's, but in spite of certain lurid flaws his best writing remains immensely effective.

The circumstances of his life had much to do with the eventual nature of his writing, and even explain some of the variations in its quality. His father, Benjamin, a self-made Chicago businessman, was gifted at making money; his mother, Gertrude, had at one point flirted with a stage career, and had cultural tastes that made the money welcome. From his birth, in Chicago in 1870, Norris had what were known as the "advantages." When the

5

family pulled up roots and moved to San Francisco, in 1884, Benjamin Norris went into real estate and did even better. But San Francisco was not to be enough for the children of Gertrude: in 1887, after vicissitudes that included the death of a brother, and a brief and unsuccessful stay in London, young Norris found himself studying art at the celebrated Académie Julien, in Paris. He was barely seventeen.

How much of the lush Paris of those years Frank Norris saw is problematical. For a year his family was also in the city; then they returned to the States and for a few months young Frank was alone — until his practical father, discovering that his son was writing tales of medieval knights instead of working at his art classes, summoned him home. The son obediently matriculated at the University of California.

He seems to have learned little about French literature during his stay in Paris. Instead, he had been intensely caught up by a sort of romantic medievalism: the lore of chivalry, armory, and the antique hardware of the Musée de Cluny. The writing that had displeased his father had been sketches concocted for his younger brother. Nothing shows that he read, say Zola, let alone any representative of the then flourishing French Symbolists. But at least he must have learned to read French.

At the University of California he assumed the role of a *boulevardier*, but not so thoroughly as to separate him from the somewhat strenuous undergraduate life of the Berkeley of that time. He joined a fraternity, and sometimes took part in the hazings and rushes he would later defend as proper training for muscular and blond young Anglo-Saxons. It appears that a chronic estrangement from the most elementary mathematics prevented his taking a degree, but he did, during his college years, pick up the ideas about human evolution, more Spencerian than Darwinian, that are reflected in his novels.

6

Meanwhile his parents had divorced, so that Norris was relieved of all pressure from his father to take up a business career. He went east, entered Harvard as a special student, and came under the benign influence of Lewis E. Gates. The Harvard English Department was ambivalently disposed toward the teaching of "creative" writing. Some members, Gates among them, obviously believed that the subject could be taught. Others followed Irving Babbitt (whose appointment was actually in French) in declaring that teaching men how to say things before they had anything to say was so much poppycock.

Norris was grateful for Gates's encouragement, and doubtless also for the incentive to work regularly. He had already begun to write: his stories had appeared in the undergraduate magazine at Berkeley, and he had had a contribution or so in the San Francisco *Wave*. More important, he had been working on the opening chapters of *McTeague*. Gates, who was familiar with continental literature, was in a position to see what he was trying to do. Clearly the stay in Paris was belatedly having an effect: Norris had been reading Zola. *McTeague* showed the influence, as did *Vandover and the Brute*, which Norris began work on in Cambridge. Although he would finish neither during the year in Cambridge, he appears to have kept both novels going at once.

Norris was taken far more by Emile Zola's individual example than by French naturalism as a whole. Although he later professed enthusiastic admiration for Flaubert, the naturalistic current that originates in the latter's *Education sentimentale*, and is transmitted by the Goncourt brothers to writers like Joris-Karl Huysmans, apparently left him untouched. Doubtless he was temperamentally unable to accept Flaubert's principle that the essence of most lives is their sheer monotony. All Norris' own novels are so full of action that one can hardly imagine his grasping the notion that monotony can be the matter of fiction. He had no perception of the great truth, so clear to all the naturalists including Zola, that both monotony and horror are mitigated by the presence of a style.

Americans rarely perceive the stylist in Zola, and Norris was no exception. The creator of the Rougon-Macquart series spent hours listening to the speech of working people, learning their special vocabularies and the unique language of each trade. Hence the rare quality of the *discours indirect libre,* or "reported speech," in which he makes his characters think. Norris, on the other hand, merely makes his characters sound ignorant, without catching the flavor and quality of what they say that would do so much to admit the reader to their lives.

He was more aware of the theoretical background of Zola's naturalism, but can hardly be said to have been impressed by it. Positivistic determinism, and the influence of heredity and environment, play only a small role in *McTeague* and a yet smaller one in *Vandover.* Norris does remember, in *McTeague,* to attribute his hero's regression to a strain of alcoholism in the family, but there is not even this to explain the decline of Vandover, whose trouble would be described by any puritanical moralist as a weakness of character.

There are grounds for wondering whether Norris ever really understood the nature of French naturalism at all. Naturalism, he argues in one of his later critical pieces, is the opposite of realism. The latter, he says, is occupied with the everyday behavior we encounter in our usual lives, whereas naturalism is concerned with the unusual and extraordinary, with life on a social level unfamiliar to us, or with happenings unlikely to occur in life as we know it. The formulation sounds strangely like Hawthorne's famous distinction between romance and novel, but Norris is thinking here of Zola: he cites as an example the incident in *La Débâcle* where a soldier discovers that he has bayoneted his old and dear comrade in arms. Norris simply mistakes Zola's idiosyn-

8

cratic penchant toward melodrama for the characterizing trait of naturalism as a whole.

Yet if Norris had not read Zola, *McTeague, Vandover,* and, later, *The Octopus* would surely not be the novels they are. If the manuals are stretching a point in making him the prime importer of naturalism into America, it is still entirely true that he is the link between our local naturalism and one of the great exponents of the French variety.

In college he had been exposed to a peculiarly American version of the theory of evolution. Starting from the brute beast, man has risen to the level where he now is, civilized, capable of intellection, possessing what may be thought of as a soul. There is reason to hope that he will continue to evolve, always upward, toward new heights. But this applies to man in the mass. In each individual there is something of the primordial beast, latent but still alive, and if anything goes wrong evolution may easily reverse its direction and the civilized being regress toward the original, brutal condition of the race. This is what happens to McTeague and Vandover.

The theory is alien to Zola's determinism; its optimism — man is headed for a greater good, while at the same time evil in individuals is explained and justified — is more intense than any that Zola or his contemporaries ever achieved. But at the same time it lends itself to the adoption of Zola's favorite literary techniques.

Minute scholarship has revealed numerous incidents and scenes in Norris' novels that are suggestive of Zola, and more particularly of *La Terre* and *La Bête humaine,* which were the novels Norris particularly preferred. But Norris' debt is greater than the total of reminiscences and borrowings. The shape of his best novels, taken as wholes, suggests that Zola's practice was never far from his mind.

The plot of *McTeague* conforms to the traditional naturalist pattern. All the needed data are given at the start, and the main action — except the ending — flows out of the data; no fact is withheld to allow the story to take an unexpected twist, and the facts given mean what they purport to mean.

McTeague would be an ordinary working man except that he has learned dentistry by watching an itinerant charlatan. He sets up his "parlors" in San Francisco, falls in love with one of his patients, and shortly marries her, but in getting Trina he makes an enemy of another suitor, Marcus Schouler. The latter reports him for practicing without a license and the state shuts his office. The loss of his livelihood sets off a decline; he takes to drink; a streak of sadism comes to the fore; he tortures his wife to make her tell him where she keeps the $5000 she has won in a lottery. She refuses, having herself become a victim of the avarice that has always been her great weakness. Finally McTeague kills her, takes the money, and returns as a fugitive to the mining country in the Sierras where he started life.

Nothing in all this seems unlikely; the story was in fact suggested by newspaper accounts of a particularly squalid murder in a poor section of San Francisco. Less likely are the two prominent subplots. In one of these a man who has married a crazy Mexican girl for the totally imaginary gold plate she keeps saying she has inherited finally slits her throat in a fit of lust for gold. And all the while an elderly couple who live in the same lodging house as the McTeagues and the other pair indulge in a somewhat mawkish, evening-of-life romance. But these are minor, and detract less from the main story than from Norris' reputation for good taste — unless, indeed, the old-age idyll is in the novel as a propitiatory sop to the bad taste of the novelist's contemporaries. The main line of the story, in any case, is up to the naturalist standard of plausibility.

The characters of *McTeague* are working people and the life Norris paints is that of the working class. Like Zola he has documented his work by direct observation; his book is not only a "novel of San Francisco" but more specifically one about life on Polk Street. He knows his Polk Street well enough to give the effect of telling the truth about what one of his successors in naturalism, James T. Farrell, calls "the exact content of life in given circumstances." The story moves in and out of the eating joints, bars, and houses, among a mixed population of poor wage-earners, some of whom are underprivileged immigrants like the girl McTeague marries.

Such a world encourages violence. Two messy murders, sundry beatings, a case of mayhem, McTeague's torturing of Trina, and the fight in the desert that ends in the death of both McTeague and Marcus combine to make *McTeague* a much more violent book than many produced by Norris' French model. And in contrast with his American contemporaries, Norris is quite willing to show his reader physical damage. There had been violence, and to spare, in earlier American writing, including *The Red Badge of Courage*; but whereas a writer like Crane tends to deflect his reader's eye from the effects of violence — the most we know of Jim Conklin's mortal wound, for example, is that it looks as if he had been chewed by wolves — Norris resolutely shows us what has happened.

Sex, on the other hand, he treats with a reticence that Zola would hardly have understood. In one episode McTeague kisses Trina "grossly" on the mouth while she is anesthetized in his dental chair; later in the book, Trina spreads her hoard of gold pieces on her bed and lies down naked on the coins; but having made clear that his characters are moved by powerful, and sometimes perverse, sexual drives, Norris is content to let the matter rest. This was doubtless as much as the American public would have permitted. The changes in taste that have intervened in the last seventy years should not be allowed to obscure the fact that even this incomplete explicitness, like indeed his finding the materials of a story in the life of the working class, was new and bold.

In making *McTeague* a case history, also, Norris was not necessarily following his French masters. Even though Zola and the Goncourts exploited this pattern repeatedly, it is also implicit in the notions of evolution he picked up in college: something goes wrong in the individual's life, the beast within emerges, and regression is inevitable. Norris did not need Zola to tell him this, and it may even be that encountering an already familiar idea when he turned his undergraduate attention on French naturalism merely deepened an existing commitment.

Nothing, of course, inhibited his following Zola closely in the use of symbols. The outsize replica of a tooth McTeague hangs outside his parlors plays the same role as the still in *L'Assommoir*, the coal-pit tower in *Germinal*, or the locomotive in *La Bête humaine*: it sums up and interprets his life. He has wanted the tooth obsessively, and is completely content once he has got it; having to give it up again represents the total shock of his catastrophe, whereas the gilt that covers it symbolizes the consuming greed for money that grows on all the principals as the story moves toward its end.

By and large Norris was right in inscribing his wife's copy of one of his novels "from the boy Zola." By itself, *McTeague* would justify the quip. Yet if there is much of Zola in this story there is even more of Norris. Between the son of the real-estate magnate and the poor mine-boy who turns dentist the social gap is wide. However interested Norris may be in such characters, they are not his kind of people. He is incapable of the sympathy that so often allowed the socialist Zola to see life as it looked to his characters; and the benign detachment of the Goncourts, explicable only by their unthinking, perhaps totally unconscious acceptance of European class distinctions, is unavailable. In America all men are created equal, but all men are not equally admissible to membership in a fraternity on the Berkeley campus. His preference for white and Protestant, Anglo-Saxon characters, almost blatant in his later novels, is already in evidence; his treatment of the ways and speech of Trina Sieppe's German immigrant family sounds at times like condescending parody.

Yet at the same time, a number of the changes Norris made in his manuscript before publication seem intended to increase his reader's liking for McTeague. Particularly in the last few chapters, when the murderous brute has become a pitiable, hunted creature, our sympathy is intended to reach out to him. And he is never mean or treacherous. Norris does not excuse his weaknesses by a sentimental appeal to overpowering environmental circumstances, but he does not condemn him, either. The trouble is that the part of the story where we are most expected to feel sympathy is also by far the one hardest to believe. The attempt fails, in large part because *McTeague* is the work of an inexperienced and still clumsy writer.

The clumsiness and inexperience show up even in passages of undeniable power. In the following, the dentist and his friends have been out on a picnic, and what began as a friendly wrestling match between McTeague and his one-time crony, Marcus, has suddenly turned into a real fight, with Marcus biting through his opponent's ear.

Then followed a terrible scene. The brute that in *McTeague* lay so close to the surface leaped instantly to life, monstrous, not to be resisted. He sprang to his feet with a shrill and meaningless clamor, totally unlike the ordinary bass of his speaking tones. It was the hideous yelling of a hurt beast, the squealing of a wounded elephant. He framed no words; in the rush of high-pitched sound that issued from his wide-open mouth there was nothing articulate. It was something no longer human; it was rather an echo from the jungle.

Sluggish enough and slow to anger on ordinary occasions,

McTeague when finally aroused became another man. His rage was a kind of obsession, an evil mania, the drunkenness of passion, the exalted and perverted fury of the Berserker, blind and deaf, a thing insensate.

As he rose he caught Marcus's wrist in both his hands. He did not strike, he did not know what he was doing. His only idea was to batter the life out of the man before him, to crush and annihilate him upon the instant. Gripping his enemy in his enormous hands, hard and knotted, and covered with a stiff fell of yellow hair — the hands of the old-time car-boy — he swung him wide, as a hammer-thrower swings his hammer. Marcus's feet flipped from the ground, he spun through the air about McTeague as helpless as a bundle of clothes. All at once there was a sharp snap, almost like the report of a small pistol. Then Marcus rolled over and over upon the ground as McTeague released his grip; his arm, the one the dentist had seized, bending suddenly, as though a third joint had formed between wrist and elbow. The arm was broken.

The young novelist's inexorable repetitiousness is part of a consciously adopted technique. From the beginning the motifs of physical size, blond or yellow hair, huge hands, strength, and sub-human stupidity have been constantly present. The passage merely expands the subject of his overwhelming animality. This insistence, rather than the occasional remarks about a theoretical determinism scattered through the early chapters, is what prepares us for McTeague's eventual reversion to the brute.

To other, more sophisticated techniques, Norris is almost aggressively indifferent. He is not in the least interested in "showing" as opposed to "telling." His immense willingness to comment on the action, to explain the cause of everything that happens — as when he tells us what the man's voice sounded like — is more pronounced here than it will be in the later novels, although he will never rid himself of it entirely. The same is true of his use of a third-person, omniscient point of view, giving himself a clear view into the mind of any character he likes and thus putting himself in the perilous position of reporting the motivations of conduct that the reader might better be trusted to deduce from behavior.

It has probably required little more than this to undermine Norris' reputation among twentieth-century critics. The enormous weight of preference for the novel according to Henry James, with its severe restriction of point of view to the "central moral consciousness," has put older and simpler procedures in a poor light. Everything in the complaints of adverse judges like Lionel Trilling and the late Joseph Warren Beach in their dismissals of the novels of Dreiser is equally applicable to Norris. The particular impact of *McTeague* cannot be accounted for by the Jamesian calculus, nor will it be admitted by critics who do not concede the occasional aesthetic effectiveness of massive accumulations of detail.

McTeague opens with a typical Sunday afternoon in the life of the hero — his dinner, his pitcher of steam beer, his nap in his own dental chair. Then comes a turn-back to his youth in the mines and to his time with the charlatan who taught him his trade. Next there is a minute description of his physique, and another of his office, including a first mention of the symbolic gilded tooth. Only after this does the novel move outside for a description of life in Polk Street. Finally, McTeague spots his chum and future nemesis, Marcus, and the first episode, the taking of a dog to a veterinary hospital, ensues. The reader has, so to speak, been given a detailed view of the habitat and the habits of the animal McTeague, and been prepared to watch the animal perform.

Such procedures may properly be called Zolaesque, since Zola used them, but they are not necessarily naturalistic in every case. Norris learned much from Zola that Zola had learned from his own predecessors. It is a naturalist strategy to give the reader all the necessary data, as *McTeague* does, at the beginning and then let the ensuing action flow out of these data, withholding nothing that could allow the story to take an unexpected twist, and making the data mean exactly what they purport to mean. But the device of showing the animal in his minutely described habitat was standard literary technique; Zola doubtless learned it from Balzac. Consequently it is fair to say that *McTeague* is a naturalistic novel, but in the sense that Zola's are naturalistic: an excellent example of nineteenth-century realism, but with special emphasis on the biological and the deterministic. Through Zola Norris got the instruments for attempting a slice of American life, seen steadily and whole. Historically, the fact that it was offered to a public whose pabulum consisted of romances like *When Knighthood Was in Flower* and the output of F. Marion Crawford imparts an additional significance.

Vandover and the Brute must be judged with greater caution. The manuscript came to light well after Norris' death. Norris may have been unwilling to publish it, or, more likely, may have been unable to find a publisher. His brother Charles revised the manuscript, although qualified opinion today holds that the latter probably did not supply the ending, as was once thought to be the case. What Norris' own feelings about the book, as we know it, would have been is a matter for speculation, at best.

Yet Norris' hero, this time, is remarkably like the author, and whereas the things that befall McTeague could not conceivably happen to people of the novelist's own kind, what happens to Vandover certainly could do so. This novel attempts a study of a representative of the San Francisco middle class, and for his naturalistic documentation Norris appears to have turned to his own autobiography.

Young Vandover returns to San Francisco with a Harvard education of sorts and the intention of developing his talent in painting. Somehow he never gets started, and the tendency to frivol away his time grows on him. He becomes more and more devoted to "vice" and "bestial pleasures," and at length seduces a girl who offers little resistance but who commits suicide when she finds herself pregnant. This event sets off a chain reaction: Vandover loses the "nice" girl he has never quite got round to marrying; Vandover's father dies; the dead girl's family brings a suit; the distraught Vandover allows himself to be cheated out of his property by an old friend of Harvard days; he gambles away what little is left, and finally his sanity wavers and collapses; he becomes a case of lycanthropy.

Lycanthropy is a mental condition in which a man thinks that he is a wolf, and behaves like one. The state is relatively rare, although well enough known to have appealed to the imaginations of certain French romantics like the poet Pétrus Borel. Few of Norris' readers can ever have seen a case, and doubtless some learn of the disease by reading his story. But the lycanthropic state, as Vandover experiences it, sounds hideous, and we cannot help wondering just what depths of vice, debauchery, and bestial pleasure brought it on.

Vandover's essays in sin seem, on the whole, rather mild and even timid. One can imagine the memory of them making a tenderly nurtured individual somewhat neurotic and guilt-ridden, but hardly anything worse. We must, of course, allow for the inhibitions imposed by the taste of the moment. The record shows, for instance, that Norris' publisher, Doubleday, wanted him to rewrite the passage in *McTeague* where "Little Owgooste," forced to sit too long while his family watches a variety show, wets his pants. If current notions of delicacy made this humble incident unpalatable to cultivated taste, what chance would there have been of describing explicitly any sort of riot among the fleshpots?

Norris' difficulty was that he was trying to follow a French model in a climate where it was impossible to do so. Zola, like the Goncourts, had been devoted to case histories of the more picturesque sort, and Norris' choice of lycanthropy is surely worthy of the master. But although Zola may have put off some readers by creating, for example, a character whose major accomplishment was the loudness of his farting, he clearly did not alienate the reading public at large, or dismay his publisher. And the direct picturing of monumental debauches in novels like *Nana* being permitted, the decline and fall of characters like Nana herself is fully motivated; the reader is not left casting about for the reason. This fact measures the distance then separating Paris from New York.

But why should Norris himself not have seen the disproportion between sin and retribution? One can only propose a plausible hypothesis. Vandover's trajectory is remarkably like the young novelist's own: origins in San Francisco; sojourn in the more sophisticated East; return — imminent in Norris' case when he was starting *Vandover* — to California with the intention of living a life that by local standards was abnormal. Whereas Vandover will paint, Norris intends to write, and neither will involve himself in ordinary ways of earning a living. If, when he got home, Norris should be unable to settle down and justify his mother's faith in his talent, then what disaster might not lie ahead? If *Vandover and the Brute* is read as transposed fantasy of this sort, the issue of plausibility does not arise.

Such a reading, on the other hand, is an invitation to the amateur psychoanalyst. What was the effect on Norris of being brought up by this strong-willed woman whose commitment to the life of the spirit — even though it took the genteel form of organizing Browning Clubs — was real enough so that she would let him live a writer's financially precarious life? And would not an explicitly documented career in sin reveal a knowledge that might desecrate the relationship of mother and son? Such questions have their special interest, even their fascination. But answering them would be an exercise in pure speculation.

Norris' biographer, Franklin Walker, was persuaded that heneath his superficial sophistication, Norris had a strong streak of puritanism in him, that within the morally noncommittal naturalist there lurked a hidden but severely disapproving moralist. This is not impossible. And the preference Norris shows in his less serious fictions for clean-minded, two-fisted, asexual but vigorous heroes tends to support the view. He was, after all, the contemporary of the founders of Boy Scouting and of the hit-the-line-hard ethics of the first Roosevelt. *Vandover* has moments when it sounds like *Stover at Yale.*

The most alert of Norris' interpreters, Donald Pizer, proposes an even simpler solution: lycanthropy is a possible stage on the way to paralytic insanity related to paresis. Pizer may be right. Paresis results from the presence of spirochetes in the bloodstream. Assuming that Norris knew this fact, he may have been trying to say, as plainly as the prevalent taboo on mentioning syphilis would let him, that his hero's escapades had left him the victim of venereal disease. But if this was what the novelist intended, all literary difficulties are not automatically removed. If Norris is saying subtly that his man is syphilitic, it must also be admitted that such subtlety is anything but characteristic. In fact, it would be hard to catch Norris being so subtle anywhere else in his collected works. And even if this instance is the exception that proves the rule, so far as the technique of fiction is concerned, it leaves Norris still in the predicament of having obscured the pivotal motivation of Vandover's story. Easiest of all the explanations to accept would be precisely that Norris did not publish the book — except for some isolated chapters — because he felt that the problem had not been solved.

Vandover is thus a flawed book; it is not an uninteresting one and has a charm unexpected in naturalist fiction. The opening descriptions of life at Harvard are worthy forerunners of classics, some of them forgotten, like George Weller's *Not to Eat; Not for*

Love. And there are period pieces, picturing the gay blades of the nineties, that stand by themselves. If Vandover's downfall could only have been made more convincing this novel might not have been dwarfed, as it is, by *McTeague*.

Norris was not so persuaded, it must appear, as we are today that in *McTeague* and *Vandover* he had found his natural manner. He went through a brief period when he abandoned his first, instinctive ways in an effort to please the genteel. But eventually, late in 1899 — thus after *Moran of the Lady Letty*, *A Man's Woman*, and *Blix* — he returned to "straight naturalism with all the guts." The expression is one he used in a letter to his friend Isaac Marcosson to tell him about his "Epic of the Wheat," of which the first volume would be *The Octopus*.

The example of Zola shows up as plainly in *The Octopus* as it does in *McTeague* or *Vandover*, but in a different way. The earlier novels had each focused on one character and the vicissitudes he passes through when his congenital weakness becomes dominant. In this respect, they suggest the relatively unadventurous Zola of novels like, say, *Son Excellence Eugène Rougon*. The Wheat trilogy, on the other hand, recalls the Zola of the great social frescoes like *Germinal* and the sprawling poems of fecundity like *La Terre* and *La Faute de l'Abbé Mouret* — the militant enemy of social abuses who combined his crusading prose with a deeply neo-pagan poetry in praise of elemental life.

Norris had planned a cyclical work, with three stories less closely interrelated than those in the Rougon-Macquart series, but treating closely related subjects. *The Octopus* describes the raising of the grain; *The Pit* continues with the buying and selling of it; and the third volume was to have been devoted to its distribution overseas. Norris died (in 1902) before he could start the third. We have only *The Octopus* and *The Pit*; and by common consent the former is greatly the better of the two, because Norris' knowledge of the machinery of business was too small, or else his feeling for business as an epic force was not intense enough. *The Octopus* may also be a better job than *McTeague*, because of its superiority in design and in articulation, but this is not generally conceded. And yet, for a number of years, *The Pit* consistently outsold these other novels and presumably had more readers. This may be for no more obscure reason than that *The Pit* has a tycoon for a hero.

In the center of *The Octopus*, like the mine in *Germinal*, is the railroad, pushing out its tracks like tentacles across California and squeezing to death everything it touches. The story is based upon an actual incident in the history of the Southern Pacific, and denounces an abuse that really existed, a system of preferential freight rates designed to extract every penny the traffic would bear.

Yet although Norris met people like Ida M. Tarbell during his months in New York, he hardly qualifies as a dedicated muckraker. He is not against Big Business on principle, and he seems even to have admired the successful business figures of his time. His disposition is more reminiscent of American Populism: when respectable, middle-class people like himself are suddenly required to wrestle with a colossus, his sympathies are on their side.

The country people in *The Octopus* have been farming land leased from the railroad, with the option eventually to buy, and have made a profit up to the time when the railroad first raises rates and then calls in the options; the price charged for the land, out of all proportion to its value at the time the farmers originally took over, is based on the value of the property after it has been improved by the farmers themselves, at their own expense. The wheat ranchers finally revolt, meet the posse sent to evict them in a pitched battle along an irrigation ditch. Those who are not killed are ruined.

The other major force in the story, along with the soulless and inhuman corporation, is the wheat itself. In a way, the heroine is the fecund American earth. Norris' long descriptions of the sowing, germination, cultivation, and harvest are without parallel in American literature; one has to go to Tolstoi for anything to rival them. Not even the bad agricultural methods of the ranchers — whom Norris does not defend for having taken too much from the earth too rapidly and without putting enough back — can exhaust this natural wealth. And in a sense the real crime of the railroad is to have frustrated nature by making it impossible for men to go on feeding other men with the wheat. By its neo-pagan adoration of nature as force, no less than by its broad canvases, the size of its landscapes and of the events that take place in them, *The Octopus* is a very Zolaesque book.

That this has not been fully recognized simply attests that criticism has been more attentive to Zola's theoretical utterances than to his practice, and is relatively unaware of how much more Zola owed to the causal theories of Hippolyte Taine than the debt he acknowledged. Zola's pronouncements sound as if the whole key to his notion of the "experimental" novel were Taine's Introduction to his *History of English Literature*, in which Taine posits a narrowly biological basis for his determinism. It happens that this Introduction was meant to catch the attention of a general reading public, at the cost of being relatively sensational in the statement of Taine's beliefs, and is peppered with such dicta as "Vice and virtue are chemical products, like sulphuric acid and sugar." In a letter written somewhat later in life, Taine remarked that he wished to God he had never written some of these capsule formulations.

Earlier than the Introduction he had written a much less flamboyant and sensational statement of his theory in a book called *Les Philosophes classiques*. Here he outlines a system of causality in which the essential notion is one of impersonal forces underlying the working of nature. Although his illustrations are biological — as they are in the Introduction — it is clear that forces of another kind, for example social or economic, are not logically excluded. With respect to this fundamental perception, the famous formula of heredity, environment, and historical moment that Taine propounds in the Introduction constitutes a grouping into categories of certain impersonal forces. Later in Taine's career, especially after 1870, he tends to emphasize forces that are social or even political. In Zola's novels, though not in his theoretical declarations, fascination with impersonal force is recognizable everywhere.

Seen in this perspective, the central subject of *The Octopus* is one that Zola would not have disowned. Mere men are powerless to change the course either of the growth of wheat or of the economic operations of the railroad. Both are impersonal, and both obey their own internal laws. (Hence the argument of one of the railroad officials that a corporation operates according to laws that cannot be changed, or their effect mitigated, by the members.)

But an impersonal force in itself is difficult to deal with in a work of literature. It must be concretized, either in a representative character or in a transparent symbol. One cannot well hate or love a legal entity, but one can discharge all kinds of emotion upon the figure of S. Behrman, the crass and repulsive agent of the carrier who also personifies the evil within it. And one can be frightened and revolted by an octopus.

The locomotive that nearly hits the young poet, Presley, in the opening chapter, is less a machine than a symbol of malevolent power.

He had only time to jump back upon the embankment when, with a quivering of all the earth, a locomotive, single, unattached, shot by him with a roar, filling the air with the reek of hot oil, vomiting smoke and sparks; its enormous eye, Cyclopean, red, throwing a glare far in advance, shooting by in a sudden crash of

23

confused thunder; filling the night with the terrific clamour of its iron hoofs. . . .

Then, faint and prolonged, across the levels of the ranch, he heard the engine whistling for Bonneville. Again and again, at rapid intervals in its flying course, it whistled for road crossings, for sharp curves, for trestles; ominous notes, hoarse, bellowing, ringing with the accents of menace and defiance; and abruptly Presley saw again, in his imagination, the galloping monster, the terror of steel and steam, with its single eye, Cyclopean, red, shooting from horizon to horizon; but saw it now as the symbol of a vast power, huge, terrible, flinging the echo of its thunder over all the reaches of the valley, leaving blood and destruction in its path; the leviathan, with tentacles of steel clutching into the soil, the soulless Force, the iron-hearted Power, the monster, the Colossus, the Octopus.

This passage could be used to show that Norris was not an accomplished stylist. The metaphors, in particular, will not survive even the friendliest scrutiny: the leviathan does not have tentacles, and the octopus, who does have them, does not use them for clutching the soil; the whistles of steam locomotives did not bellow. This frightening Thing undergoes too many metamorphoses in a brief space just so that we will be frightened by it. But it is less important that he should be denounced for straining after effect than that he should have felt the straining necessary. The symbol must be established, by all the resources of rhetoric he can muster. This is the elevated style of a period that found its models in the emphatic improvisations of political and pulpit eloquence, but it is nonetheless an elevated style. Norris is calling upon it to confer importance upon a symbol which will give us something we can really hate.

By a similar process, S. Behrman, the agent, is made similarly useful. There is no causal connection between Behrman's job and his insensitiveness, his grotesque taste in dress, his crude manners. He could serve the company as well if he were blessed by the opposite qualities. But the reader can detest this man, with his varnished straw hat and his vest covered with embroidered horseshoes, and through him the organization he serves. There is supposed to be poetic justice in the accident at the end of the story, when Behrman is killed by the wheat. He personifies a force, and must be killed by a force. His presence, like the recurring symbol of the locomotive, connects the principal line of the story with the tradition of naturalism.

Just as in *McTeague*, however, Norris' naturalism is not unrelieved. Interwoven with the main action are a number of subplots that cannot by any stretch be called naturalist.

Presley has come to the wheat-growing San Joaquin Valley to write a long poem about the land and its Spanish past. Before the year is out he gives up the project in favor of a poem about the here and now, and the realities of life in the Valley; it attacks the trusts. His role in the novel is to provide the point of view of an educated and refined sensibility. Norris does not use him, as Henry James would have done, as the consciousness through whom all the action is refracted. We see the events from his angle only upon occasion. But his sensitive responses to them allow Norris to avoid some of the commentary he might otherwise have felt impelled to insert, and at the same time the story of what happens to his poem forms an implicit commentary on the conflict between the major forces in contention.

Presley's friend Vanamee, the sheep-herding mystic, has little connection with the principal thread of the novel except that his sheep are the ones run down by the locomotive in the first chapter. He prefers solitude and stays aloof from the concerns of the ranchers. Years before, his one true love had been brutally raped by some unknown, and then died after childbirth. By some extrasensory means that is never explained beyond calling it a concentration of mental energy, he believes that he can bring her

25

back. Vanamee, rather than the Mexican parish priest who is included only for local color, appears to represent the spiritual in a situation where the other characters are overwhelmingly preoccupied with the material: for the farmers, engrossed in their struggle for life, a devotion like his would be unthinkable.

For us, on the other hand, the event it produces is unbelievable. Feeling that his dead fiancée is drawing nearer, Vanamee takes to waiting for her in a mission garden, and finally she does indeed come, over the new wheat — in the person of the now-grown child who looks exactly like her. The reader is expected to believe that she has lived in this country neighborhood since her birth without Vanamee's having heard the least rumor of it.

In another subplot, the rancher Annixter, a crabbed health-faddist with marked misogynistic leanings, is attracted to the young and wholesome Hilma Tree, the dairymaid. When she rejects the chance to become his mistress, Annixter discovers that the strange stirrings within him must be love. He proposes marriage and is accepted; they spend their honeymoon in San Francisco, and by the time when, after their return, Annixter is killed in the battle by the irrigation ditch, we have been persuaded that love of a fine woman has made him a better man. The touch of Dickensian sentimentality is less obtrusive than the idyll of the old couple in *McTeague*, probably because Annixter is one of the harried ranchers and thus plays another role in the story besides that of hero in a love affair.

A fourth subplot involves one Dyke, an engineer who loses his job with the railway, then finds himself forced off his farm, tries to meet his desperate need for money by robbing a train, kills a trainman, and is finally hunted down as a fugitive. All Dyke has ever wanted is to give his little daughter a decent education in a seminary for young ladies.

Thus while in its main lines *The Octopus* has much of the typical naturalist novel, much else in it does not conform to the naturalist pattern. From episode to episode the railroad wins and the farmers lose; force crashes against force with the inevitable outcome. Courts, legislature, posses combine to crush the hopeless individuals. And when all is finished we are shown examples of the wrecked lives of the dispersed farmers. But this in itself does not account for the subplots to which Norris has clearly given much attention.

After *The Octopus, The Pit* is a disappointment. Norris did not know Chicago as he knew the land and people of California, and what he knew about trading in wheat futures was not enough to fill a book. The second installment of his epic accordingly shrinks to the dimensions of a domestic love story.

The hero, Curtis Jadwin, has made one fortune in real estate and appears about to make another in wheat. He marries a genteelly cultivated girl from New England and installs her in a luxurious mansion near the Lake. They move in a society that justifies Henry James's complaint that America is socially too poor and thin to support a novel. Laura Jadwin's efforts to refine her husband do not succeed, and his success at the Exchange enflames his gambling instinct. While he is busy trying to corner the world's supply, she is very tempted to run off with a former suitor, the effete aesthete Corthell. Jadwin is ruined when his corner breaks. The marriage barely survives.

Norris revives his usual devices. The book is built around the familiar recurrent symbol — in this case the metaphor of the Wheat Pit as a gigantic whirlpool — shored up by his most ambitious prose. He invokes the economic law of supply and demand, and the natural law that when men are hungry more food will be planted, to play the roles of impersonal forces. Although *The Pit* is not so complex and heavily populated as *The Octopus*, he is still working in broad, panoramic frescoes. There is even a hint of

Jadwin's decline under adversity, but its course is arrested by the presence of a good woman.

For once a Norris novel has a fully realized, if not completely winning, heroine. One suspects the brunette and slight Laura Jadwin is a composite of his mother, Gertrude Norris, and Jeannette Black Norris, his wife. She is, in any case, no mere love-object of a muscularly masculine hero, but is treated as interesting in her own right: a very considerable share of the novel is given over to her story, from Massachusetts to Chicago and from girlhood through marriage to neglect, temptation, and final reconciliation. Unfortunately, Norris also makes her self-centered and occasionally downright selfish. But despite her shallowness she is real and, in Norris' world, new.

Jadwin, on the other hand, is a close relative of McTeague. A tycoon born on the farm, one of the generation whose wealth did not inhibit their liking to sit out on the "front stoop" on warm spring evenings, he has the powerful muscles, awkwardness, and ineradicable lack of polish of the working man. With him is contrasted Corthell, who represents "art" while Jadwin represents "life"; there is no doubting Norris' preference for the energetic and still primitive philistine over the pallid man of refinement.

For Norris is faithful to the clichés of his age. A man who gets to the top of the pile does so by virtue of superior qualities of energy and strength. Social Darwinism here supports the Protestant ethic. Society is not inherently bad, but it encourages frivolity and the cultivation of the less virile qualities of character. Cities are interesting but corrupt, while strength of character comes from contact with the land and the elements.

Norris' critical essays, perfunctory and sketchy as many of them are, reveal a hard core of anti-intellectualism, with the characteristically American contradiction that consists of respect for and, simultaneously, suspicion of education. They contain no seriously articulated notion of the purpose and value of the literary activity to which he has nonetheless committed his own life, but declare repeatedly that "life" is better than "art." Jadwin is the kind of hero he could, and did, admire.

This is why Jadwin is not a very convincing Titan. If this fundamentally simple and uningenious man could corner the world's wheat, it is hard to see why any reasonably shrewd though not especially intelligent character, given enough money, could not do the same thing — and why, indeed, it is not done with distressing regularity.

There is no escaping it: *The Pit* reveals Norris' great weakness. An inadequate understanding of human character is intimately related to the defect in his style that vitiates even the central metaphor of his book. The image of the great whirlpool strikes us as vastly overwritten simply because Jadwin's accomplishment is not so great as Norris thinks. Jadwin, himself, is not big enough and words alone will not make him so. It would not be unjust to say of his performance in *The Pit* what Lionel Trilling says of Dreiser in all his novels: he does not write well because he thinks poorly.

Hence a survey of his contribution to American naturalism must conclude that it is indeed right to call him a naturalist but that calling him one does not account fully for the whole nature of his talent. There is another, non-naturalist side to him even in his best work. When one turns to the rest, what this side was becomes unmistakable. Most of Norris' critics have dutifully noted the strain of melodrama that persistently turns up in his stories, but usually to minimize it as perhaps regrettable but not particularly important. Yet it is a constant factor in his successes (except *Vandover*) and his failures (except, perhaps, *Blix*).

Norris had gone home from Harvard, in the summer of 1895, with two unfinished novels and no immediate intention of going on with his writing. Before the year ended he was in South Africa reporting for one of the San Francisco papers on the unrest that preceded the Boer War. He was present at the fiasco of Jameson's raid, saw such excitement as there was to see, was under fire at least once, and caught a fever that put an end to any thought of further African adventure.

There followed two years of sporadic writing and journalism in San Francisco. He resumed writing for the San Francisco *Wave*, turning out sketches, essays, and some of the short stories that were posthumously collected in *The Third Circle* (1909). With renewed health came a certain tendency toward dissipation — of a rather mild sort from all appearances — and the renewed discovery that writing can be hard work. During 1897 he seems to have gone through a period of marked depression.

But in 1896 he had met Jeannette Black, and the progress of the courtship coincided with a return of creative energy. Early in 1898 Norris was writing an adventure story for publication by installments in the *Wave*. This was *Moran of the Lady Letty*. In New York, S. S. McClure had been reading Norris' incidental writings in the *Wave*, and, with the first installments of *Moran* in print, invited Norris to come to New York and take a job. McClure had joined forces with Frank Doubleday, in the house of Doubleday, McClure, and Company, by the time Norris got there.

This was how Norris came to be the editorial reader who drew the firm's attention to the manuscript of Dreiser's *Sister Carrie*. Meanwhile Doubleday and McClure published *Moran of the Lady Letty* in 1898 and *McTeague*, at last completed, in 1899. *Moran* went largely unreviewed, and *McTeague*, though praised by Howells, stirred considerable protest — there were cries of "stamp out this race of Norrises" — without raising the kind of scandal that sells books in quantity. Even Howells had suggested that Norris might do well in future to avoid the extreme realism for which we read *McTeague* today. Doubtless convinced that Howells was right, Norris went to work on *A Man's Woman*, a novel incapable of shocking any taste at all other than the purely literary. His letters show that he found the book disastrously hard to write and was perfectly aware of not having brought it off. He published it, even so, in newspaper installments during 1899 and in book form in 1900.

His one other excursion outside naturalism was *Blix*, a transposition into fiction of his romance with Jeannette Black. The hero, Condy Rivers, is a young writer who falls in love with a well-bred girl — he nicknames her "Blix" — who has little patience with the frivolity of contemporary San Francisco society. Condy has most of the amiable characteristics of a young college graduate, including a tendency to fool away time and money gambling at his club. Blix learns poker and beats him consistently, until he finally gives up the pastime. Being autobiographical well beyond the degree reached in *Vandover*, this love story adds an interesting sidelight on the latter novel: the suggestion is strong, in *Blix*, that Norris entertained private worries about going to the dogs. In the novel, as in real life, he does not do so: Blix eventually leaves for the East and Condy receives a providential invitation from an eastern publisher that will enable him to follow her.

Some critics, including the late Lars Åhnebrink, have found this novel "charming." Its accounts of the couple's walks along the edge of the Pacific, and one of a fishing expedition to an inland lake, are in fact informed by a kind of heartwarming felicity. But more significant for the present purpose are the chapters in which, on their walks, the couple fall in with the keeper of a life-saving station who has knocked about the world extensively and has a fund of stories to tell. These Condy drinks in, to store against the day when he will need them for his books. This is "material" and also contact, albeit at second hand, with "life." Condy's cultivation of this parasitical relationship suggests the importance for Norris of his own conversations with one Captain Joseph Hodgson of the Fort Point Coast Guard station.

Books of action and adventure were selling well, but Paris, Berkeley, and Harvard had prepared Norris poorly for such enterprises. However convinced he was that "life is better than literature," in this sense he had not lived. He was entirely willing to be a romancer as well as a novelist, but the competition was stiff: Stevenson, Richard Harding Davis, Kipling, and Joseph Conrad had all gone places and done things.

So had Norris, briefly. Like so many others he had been an accredited correspondent in the Spanish-American War and had seen some of the fighting, but, like his trip to South Africa, this expedition seems to have given him little to use in his fiction. Condy's attachment to "Captain Jack" suggests strongly that he felt a kind of poverty of invention in himself. Did Norris entertain the same feeling? His willingness to work with second-hand materials, like the delight he took, according to one of his letters, in the writing of *Moran*, excites suspicions of his seriousness. Was he a writer with "something to say" that gave him trouble in the saying, or was he merely a rather talented young man who wanted terribly to be a writer?

Alternative answers may be proposed. His early commitment to naturalism may have been only experimental. Or it may be that he was short of money, wanted to marry, and loved Jeannette Black more than he did any special literary mode. What is certain is that *Moran of the Lady Letty*, and even more so *A Man's Woman*, attest the fallibility of a method that capitalizes upon vicarious experience.

Moran has the distinction of being one of the best yarns about salt water and derring-do ever written by an author who knew nothing firsthand about either. Even while his novel was coming out in installments, Norris was hearing from knowledgeable friends about his howlers in nautical terminology and procedures. He seems to have listened unperturbed and was perhaps right in doing so: reviewers of his finished book were much more critical of the superabundance of unnecessary incident than of bloopers about the art of navigation. But his ignorance of his subject was not, of course, unrelated to the proliferation of episodes.

Of these there is surely God's plenty. Ross Wilbur, a San Franciscan, Yale graduate, and dedicated ladies' man, happens into a dockside saloon to while away the time between a tea and a debutante party, drinks a Mickey Finn, is dropped through a trapdoor, and finds himself shanghaied aboard a disreputable schooner manned by a Chinese crew and commanded by a white thug. They drop down the coast looking for anything they can scavenge or salvage, and meet the derelict *Lady Letty*. Aboard the drifting hulk is one living soul, a somewhat postadolescent Norse goddess, big, blonde, beautiful, and profane, but absolutely unfamiliar with men. An accident leaves her and Wilbur to command the schooner and its Chinese crew through a series of wild adventures. These include a night battle on the shore, against the crew of a marauding Chinese junk, for the possession of a piece of ambergris. Excited by the fighting until she does not know who is her enemy, the girl Moran throws herself upon Wilbur in berserk rage. He subdues her by physical force — and as he holds her helpless Moran learns to love the man who has mastered her.

When, after other and no more credible adventures, they bring their ship back to California, Wilbur has become another man. He has killed an opponent in armed combat. His muscles are hard. And at the same time he has been regenerated by the primitive maiden, and the once effete Yale man is now thoroughly out of patience with the social whirl, to which he cannot think of returning. Similarly, Moran has been changed by her contact with a

33

cultured and civilized man into a charmingly feminine, though incompletely tamed, young woman.

At this point Norris played with the idea of sending them on another voyage, this time around Cape Horn to join the filibusterers drawn to Cuba by the approach of war. This he renounced, however, in favor of having Moran murdered by a skulking Chinese crewman she and Wilbur had protected from the vengeance of an enemy tong. The choice had the obvious merit of ending the yarn and getting an inconveniently antisocial heroine off Norris', and his hero's, hands.

Moran easily sustains a first reading, though most readers would require a special incentive to undertake a second: the strain of suspending disbelief is simply too great.

A Man's Woman is no less demanding, and offers even less in the way of reward. The story involves an Arctic explorer who comes home from an expedition to the northern wastes, where most of his companions died, to claim the love of a rich woman who has turned her back on an empty social life, founded a nurses' home, and herself become a nurse. Later he forces her to abandon nursing his closest friend — a survivor of the expedition — just as the latter is at the crisis of typhoid, because he objects to her endangering herself. The friend dies, but the couple marry — and after some months the hero renounces his bliss to depart on a new expedition to the North Pole.

The heroine, Lloyd Searight, is another Moran in physique and pale Nordic beauty, but has wealth, education, and unmitigated idealism in addition. Ward Bennett, the explorer, is a McTeague in a Brooks Brothers suit: he even has the same jutting jaw and somewhat neanderthal brow. Well-born, educated, intelligent, but at the same time full of uncontrolled brute energy, he is devoted to getting exactly what he wants — the love of a woman, one last exhausted effort from companions dying on an ice floe, or the assent of his fiancée to desert a man who will perish without her aid. In the Arctic he proves himself capable of any extreme — and is no less so when he returns to civilization. When Lloyd's horse threatens to run away with her, for example, he kills the beast with one blow of his geologist's hammer.

The book presents the reader with more psychological improbabilities than he can easily tolerate. Would any man, in the name of love, insist on leaving his friend to die wretchedly for lack of nursing? Would a woman of Lloyd's alleged intelligence and pride have accepted being forced into such a situation? Would any woman with a minimum of self-respect have fallen in love with this educated gorilla in the first place? The difficulty of belief was already great in *Moran*; here it is insuperable.

The important truth about *A Man's Woman* is not so much that this novel is melodramatic as that the melodrama taken as such is of low quality. *Moran of the Lady Letty*, even more shamelessly devoted to a world divided without nuance into bad people and good people, inattentive to proportions between cause and effect, subordinating motive to action, caring little if anything about probability, and depending heavily on the reader's overlooking its defects in his eagerness to learn what happens next, is far less offensive. Norris has poor Moran murdered in cold blood simply to be rid of her. Wilbur has left her aboard the schooner moored just offshore while he does an errand in San Francisco; the one Chinese remaining with them attacks her with his knife; love has civilized her to the point where she cannot use her strength to resist; the murderer leaves her body aboard, slips the cables so that the schooner will be wrenched free at any strain, and swims ashore; the captain of the lifeboat station finds her dead and brings the news to Wilbur just as the *Lady Letty* breaks away; Wilbur can only helplessly watch his schooner standing out to sea bearing the body of his beloved into the sunset. We do not greatly object, possibly because we know that Norris, himself, did not take the book very seriously and had a huge good time writing it.

But the final chapters of *McTeague* are not just an expedient for breaking off a yarn; from the sketches submitted as "themes" in Lewis E. Gates's writing class, it is clear that they were in the original plan. His delay in finishing the book is evidence that he was not entirely sure of their fitting with the rest.

He makes poor McTeague take flight back into the Sierras, looking for safety in the scenes of his boyhood, lets him find gold he will never be able to spend, endows him with a special sixth sense that infallibly warns of danger. As the posse approaches, McTeague takes flight again down the Panamint Range and into the desert. His implacable enemy, Schouler, insists on following him alone, after the posse, which he has now joined, turns back. The chase continues through the desert, which Norris widens beyond its geographical dimensions for the purpose, until the inexorable pursuer catches up. They fight; and McTeague kills Schouler — but only after the latter, in one last surge of strength, shackles himself to McTeague with handcuffs for which there is no key. They are miles from the nearest water.

Few, even among Norris' enthusiastic admirers, argue that this abrupt change in modes of fiction enhances *McTeague*. Nevertheless, the common judgment is that the turn to a flight-and-pursuit pattern does not impair the quality of the earlier part of the novel. They are perhaps right, but the same plea cannot be made in favor of *The Octopus*, because this whole novel is structured on the principle of melodrama, and one's final judgment depends on how well one feels the melodrama succeeds.

The essence of melodrama is violent contrast, and *The Octopus* is built of violently contrasting scenes. The slaughter of Vanamee's sheep, in the opening chapter, follows the scene of quiet conversation in which the sheepherder reveals so much of himself to

Presley. The arrival of the bad news that the railroad has called in its options comes directly after the pages about the merriment of the whole ranching community at Annixter's barn dance. The sequence on Annixter's honeymoon with Hilma in San Francisco is sandwiched between accounts of how Dyke has been starved off his own land, and of how he robs the train — which happens to be the express that is bringing the couple back to the ranch. The episode of the great jack-rabbit drive and its attendant slaughter ends with the word that a posse is coming, and the ranchers hurry home to be slaughtered themselves.

There is thus no change in method toward the close of the book, when Norris adopts a technique of alternating fragments of pieces of dissociated but contrasting action. In the penultimate chapter, after disposing of various minor characters — Minna Hooven, for example, is driven to prostitution — Norris picks up, first, a dinner party at the home of one of the officials of the railroad, and, second, the wanderings of old Mrs. Hooven and six-year-old Hilda, penniless and looking for a place to sleep. The night is cold, and the woman and child are desperate; the dinner, at which Presley is surprised to find himself a guest, is elaborate and succulent. The camera switches back and forth between the dinner and the waifs in increasingly rapid rhythm, with each shot briefer than the one preceding. Finally we see the couple sink down under a bush. We return to the dinner:

Just before the ladies left the table, young Lambert raised his glass of Madeira. Turning toward the wife of the Railroad King he said:

"My best compliments for a delightful dinner."

Then back to the bench:

The doctor, who had been bending over Mrs. Hooven, rose.

"It's no use," he said; "she has been dead some time — exhaustion from starvation."

These last pages are not only immensely effective in themselves but also entirely appropriate in the structure of the novel: they accelerate the rhythm that the reader has felt from the beginning. The rapid and incessant reversals of fortune are rushed to a kind of climax. The technique is the one that would be adopted, a decade or so later, for the wordless narrations of the early movies. To describe it one is almost forced to fall back upon the vocabulary of the cinema.

The final chapter moves in a much slower tempo. The hated S. Behrman has come to watch the lading of a ship that will carry some of the railroad's surplus wheat to the starving Orient. The operation is automatic. No one else is about. By itself the golden stream pours out of a hopper and falls into the hold. Behrman loses his balance, lands in the hold with the flood pouring in upon him. He struggles against it, tries to find a ladder, screams. The wheat mounts inexorably. His struggles weaken. At the end of the sequence one sclerotic hand sticks out above the rising surface of the grain. Then the hand, too, disappears beneath the flowing gold.

This ending is almost obligatory. The logic of *The Octopus* requires this last, crowning contrast, emphasized by the slowness of the pace and the fadeout at the end. It returns us to the conflict of the great, elemental forces: the railroad has won its battle on the purely human plane; nothing can be done for victims; but in the titanic struggle in which they have been pawns the scapegoat representing the force of the corporation is overwhelmed by the force of the wheat, which is the force of nature itself.

And at the same time, Behrman's end satisfies another compelling need. The villain must not be allowed to prosper from his misdeeds. That everyone else should suffer without his being punished would violate the fundamental law of melodrama. Also, as befits melodrama, the punishment has to be ironic; it is right that Behrman should die under the weight of the wealth he has helped accumulate.

The reader has been prepared for this crowning irony from very early on. The principle underlying the contrasts of events that determines the structure is basically an ironic one. We learn very soon that whenever anything seems to be going well for any of the characters he is merely being deluded and that new misfortune will shortly come upon him. We know what the character does not — that no matter what he does to avoid it, trouble will come.

Of course, there is nothing inherently melodramatic in such irony in itself. It frequently appears in the most respected tragedy, for example the *Oedipus*. But in tragedy it is an aspect of the human condition and its presence is inevitable, whereas in melodrama it is present because someone has stacked the cards.

At his best, Norris is not greatly worried about credibility, and coincidence is endemic, not only in *Moran* and *A Man's Woman* but in the novels he took more seriously as well. McTeague's carrying his poor canary in its gilded cage through weather that would have killed a gamecock, Norris' extending the boundaries of the desert so that McTeague can get too far away from water, like Vanamee's not knowing — for all his supersensory powers — that the lost fiancée's daughter has been right there in the neighborhood, appear not to have disturbed him, and are unlikely to disturb a present-day reader. And one finds no disabling defect at the beginning of *The Octopus* when, to introduce his dramatis personae and finish rapidly with the exposition, he arranges for young Presley to meet practically every important character in the book, and hear all the local news, in the course of one afternoon's bicycle ride down the valley. But elsewhere he rigs the game precisely for the sake of irony. Bad news, we have noticed, always arrives *after* moments of joy or jollity. And of all the trains poor Dyke could have chosen to rob, he must fall on none other than the one carrying the Annixters home from their honeymoon. In such instances the relationship between cause and effect is, to say the least, incoherent.

Once the first excitement of reading has worn off, one wonders even if the death of S. Behrman was not contrived, also. The holds of ships are normally equipped with ladders. Behrman is not so stunned by his fall that he is unable to flounder about. Yet he does not flounder along the bulkhead, where the wheat would be less deep and where, even if blinded by dust, he would know that he could find a ladder by groping with his hands. Did Behrman truly die an ironic death, or was he, like Moran, simply murdered by his author?

Seen in the light of his most successful novel — which after all we must take *The Octopus* to be — Norris emerges as an instinctive melodramatist working with naturalist materials. The formula may be extended to describe the author of *McTeague*, and, in some degree, of *Vandover* and *The Pit*. It accounts for the nature of his successes and at the same time for his characteristic awkwardness in dealing with such problems as the elementary one created by the fact that a novelist is supposed to deal with live men and women.

In especial, women. Apart from the heroine of *Blix* (which, as an idyll, belongs to a special critical category) and Laura Jadwin in *The Pit*, his women are either kept in auxiliary roles, like Trina and the other feminine figures in *McTeague*, and presented in terms of one or two simple character traits, or else handled with extraordinary gingerliness. The reader would be at a loss to say, for example, what the "fast" Ida Wade, whom Vandover seduces, actually looks like. She is hardly more than an object for the momentary attention of Vandover. And Moran, although described much more completely, impresses much less as a human female than as a wish fulfillment.

Moran's long hair, statuesque body — she stands six feet, with broad hips and deep breasts — and blonde complexion may have been meant to make her look like a seagoing Brünnehilde, and his point is clear; but in her ignorance, innocence, and sexual unawareness she seems even more a statue come to life — the Galatea of a timid erotic fantasy. As a story, *Moran of the Lady Letty* needs little more than she provides, however; complexity of character, or depth, would make her presence inconvenient for the hurried romancer.

Hilma Tree, in *The Octopus*, has a much more important literary function: she is the young woman for whom Annixter, one of the central figures in the book, makes over his life. She is another tall, blonde, and opulent woman, and more amply described than any other woman in the book. But Norris simply refuses to let the reader look at her. The dominant adjectives in the descriptions — "sane," "honest," "strong," "alert," "joyous," "robust," "vigorous," "vibrant," "exuberant" — indicate only Annixter's responses to her. Doubtless the reader is expected to respond in the same way, but his impression is more likely to be that Annixter, still eccentric, has gone off the deep end for a country wench who washes her face and knows how to milk a cow. Of Lloyd Searight, the heroine of *A Man's Woman*, there is little more to say.

But while what the critics commonly report about Norris' women is undeniable, reports on his men are easily overdone. It is true that several of his heroes run to a type: evolution has produced, if we judge by them, nothing finer than the blond, strong, somewhat prognathous, perhaps a bit dumb but never inactive, Anglo-Saxon. In comparison, other races are inferior; white supremacy is axiomatic. Orientals are treacherous by nature; other foreigners can hardly be taken seriously and at times are simply comic. McTeague is a brute, but occupies a place on the evolutionary ladder on which Ross Wilbur occupies a higher rung; the latter needs only to have the social veneer worn away, and the muscular primitive beneath brought out, by a few months of buccaneering. Ward Bennett is, in Norris' eyes, the complete "man's man." Beside men like these, intellectuals and persons of advanced aesthetic taste show up badly. Even emotional sensibility seems a bit suspect: Norris is all admiration when Bennett leaves old companions to die disabled on the Arctic ice, and shows no indignation when Jadwin shrugs off the thousands who will have no bread because he has forced up the price of wheat.

Yet, especially in his later novels, a very considerable number of male characters do not conform to pattern. Aside from Jadwin himself, most of the men in *The Pit* have little of the Nordic superman about them; in *The Octopus* there are none. Annixter is a man of action when need arises, and shoots it out with the drunken cowboy Delaney when the latter tries to break up the barn dance, but as a group, he, the Derricks, and their friends are ordinary citizens. Toward the end of his life Norris may have been coming around to the idea that the common American man can be something of a hero.

Critics have been at pains to show that Norris meant to reveal, discreetly, the sexuality of his characters in such incidents as McTeague's kissing the anesthetized Trina. They are quick to concede, however, that the attempts are very discreet indeed, that at most the novelist intended only to implant the idea of sexuality in the reader's mind and leave the rest to his imagination. But, on the whole, this is not convincing. Norris not only shies away from sex, but also from most aspects of private, domestic life. One remembers only one pregnancy in his novels, that of poor Ida in *Vandover* — of course a bad thing that brings its own punishment. Among Laura Jadwin's complaints, which after several years of married life are not few, there is no mention of her being child-less. One is left with the uncomfortable conclusion that these women were not real enough to have children.

In any event, the population of Norris' world is too unvaried, and perhaps his understanding of life itself was not deep enough, to permit writing the kind of social and psychological novels that Henry James has taught us to prefer. Possibly because his under-standing of life itself was also melodramatic, so that he saw men and women only in melodramatic relationships, he did not feel the need. Something of the sort seems to have been his great limitation. It was only when he could bring the techniques of melodrama to deal with a subject adapted to and tolerant of the limitation that he wrote enduring work.

He had planned another "epic," which would have retold the story of Gettysburg, with one volume for each of the three days. For the ultimate judgment of his talent, it is a pity that he did not live to write it. That he was thinking of a subject that, by its nature, did not involve women suggests at least faintly that he had discovered where his bent lay. He might have suffered from the inevitable comparison with Stephen Crane, but even this would have been revealing.

Today, his novels reveal their weaknesses more strikingly than their strengths. Henry James has reformed our notion of the novel. Psychoanalysis has changed our understanding of human personality. An intervening generation of stylists and techni-cians — Hemingway, Wolfe, Fitzgerald, Faulkner — has given us a new respect for the word, and perhaps also a new suspicion of the word used carelessly. We have come to expect that a novel will offer us the spectacle of "ethics in action," and at the same time the vectors of stress in our ideas of social and personal morality point in totally different directions. Even the country Norris was writing about has changed beyond recognition. It follows that we cannot appreciate Norris' achievement unless by a vigorous, and sympathetic, effort of the historical imagination.

His better books insisted, by their example, that literature was a serious matter — in a time which, to judge by its recorded preferences, had not granted this point. His blend of naturalism and melodrama was, as Dreiser's career also testifies, as much as the country could take before the great expansion of tolerance in taste that came, not without resistance in many quarters, after 1918. We think today that it opened the way not only for Dreiser but for all the novelists who, without professing the naturalist faith, have needed the freedom in choice and treatment of subject that the naturalists were the first to claim.

In France and elsewhere, naturalism aimed to produce a kind of shock effect: the exposure of the animal behavior of the human animal was not expected to be accepted with tranquility. Naturalism was working with a new dimension of humanity, and offering a new explanation of certain puzzling aspects of human behavior. Not that Norris was, by nature, animated by a desire to shock people. But the testimony of contemporary critics of *McTeague* is convincing: their genteel rejection of the novel is evidence that it did, in fact, shock. The shock had to be achieved, and its first effect dulled, before the American novel could move into the wide field it occupies today. We can measure its potential for shock by the fact that even now, in spite of our habit-induced dullness, Norris' picture of life as actually lived in a given time and place has retained some power to shock.

Meanwhile, what V. L. Parrington called critical realism aimed, more or less consciouslessly, at exposing imperfections and abuses in society and in the political structure, often by making the reader identify himself with the victims. To the extent that *The Octopus* still arouses our sympathies for the wheat ranchers, even though the depredations of the railroads have long since become an academic matter, we have to call this novel a success.

And further, in spite of his penchant for melodrama, Norris' better novels played their part in substituting flesh and blood people for the myth-figures — the Sheriffs, Rangers, Cowboys, and such — in the literature of the American West. If we honor writers like Stephen Crane for their part in this achievement, we can hardly deny Norris the credit he, too, deserves.

⤴ Selected Bibliography

Works of Frank Norris

Yvernelle. Philadelphia: Lippincott, 1892.

Moran of the Lady Letty. New York: Doubleday and McClure, 1898.

McTeague. New York: Doubleday and McClure, 1899.

Blix. New York: Doubleday and McClure, 1899.

A Man's Woman. New York: Doubleday and McClure, 1900. (Serialized in 1899.)

The Octopus. New York: Doubleday, Page, 1901.

The Pit. New York: Doubleday, Page, 1903.

The Responsibilities of the Novelist and Other Literary Essays. New York: Doubleday, Page, 1903.

Vandover and the Brute. Garden City, N.Y.: Doubleday, Page, 1914.

Complete Edition of Frank Norris. Garden City, N.Y.: Doubleday, Doran, 1928. (Contains the works listed above, and in addition reprints Norris' short stories, Vol. IV, and journalistic writings, Vol. X.)

The Letters of Frank Norris, edited by Franklin D. Walker. San Francisco: Book Club of California, 1956.

The Literary Criticism of Frank Norris, edited by Donald Pizer. Austin: University of Texas Press, 1964. (Collects, with illuminating commentary, all Norris' important criticism.)

Current American Reprints

McTeague. New York: Holt, Rinehart, and Winston. $1.50. New York: Premier (Fawcett World). $.75. New York: Signet (New American Library). $.60.

The Octopus. New York: Bantam Books. $.75. Boston: Riverside (Houghton Mifflin). $1.25.

The Pit. New York: Evergreen (Grove). $2.95. New York: Signet, $.95.

Bibliography

Lohf, Kenneth A., and Eugene P. Sheehy, compilers. *Frank Norris: A Bibliography.* Los Gatos, Calif.: Talisman Press, 1959.

Critical and Biographical Studies

Åhnebrink, Lars. *The Beginnings of Naturalism in American Fiction.* Cambridge, Mass.: Harvard University Press, 1950.

Selected Bibliography

Biencourt, Marius. *Une Influence du naturalisme français en Amérique: Frank Norris*. Paris: Giard, 1933.

Cargill, Oscar. *Intellectual America: Ideas on the March*. New York: Macmillan, 1941. Pp. 89–107.

Chase, Richard. *The American Novel and Its Tradition*. Garden City, N.Y.: Doubleday, 1957. Pp. 185–204.

Collins, Carvel. Introduction to *McTeague*. New York: Holt, Rinehart, and Winston reprint, 1950.

Cooperman, Stanley. "Frank Norris and the Werewolf of Guilt," *Modern Language Quarterly*, 20:252–58 (September 1959).

Folsom, James K. "Social Darwinism or Social Protest? The 'Philosophy' of *The Octopus*," *Modern Fiction Studies*, 8:393–400 (Winter 1962–63).

Geismar, Maxwell. *Rebels and Ancestors*. Boston: Houghton Mifflin, 1953. Pp. 3–66.

Hicks, Granville. *The Great Tradition*. New York: Macmillan, 1933. Pp. 168–75.

Howells, William Dean. "Frank Norris," *North American Review*, 175:769–78 (December 1902).

Kazin, Alfred. *On Native Grounds*. New York: Reynal and Hitchcock, 1942. Pp. 97–102.

Lynn, Kenneth S. Introduction to *The Octopus*. Boston: Houghton Mifflin (Riverside Editions reprint), 1958.

Marchand, Ernest. *Frank Norris, a Study*. Stanford, Calif.: Stanford University Press, 1942.

Millgate, Michael. *American Social Fiction: James to Cozzens*. New York: Barnes and Noble, 1964. Pp. 38–53.

Pizer, Donald. *The Novels of Frank Norris*. Bloomington: Indiana University Press, 1966.

Taylor, Walter F. *The Economic Novel in America*. Chapel Hill: University of North Carolina Press, 1942. Pp. 282–306.

Walcutt, Charles C. *American Literary Naturalism, a Divided Stream*. Minneapolis: University of Minnesota Press, 1956. Pp. 114–56.

Walker, Franklin D. *Frank Norris: A Biography*. Garden City, N.Y.: Doubleday, Doran, 1932.